Revolutionary War Soldiers

Diane Smolinski

Series Consultant:
Lieutenant Colonel G.A. LoFaro

Heinemann Library
Chicago, Illinois

© 2002 Reed Educational & Professional Publishing
Published by Heinemann Library,
an imprint of Reed Educational & Professional
Publishing, Chicago, IL

Customer Service 888-454-2279

Visit our website at www.heinemannlibrary.com

Designed by Herman Adler Design
Printed in China

10
10 9 8 7

Library of Congress Cataloging-in-Publication Data

Smolinski, Diane, 1950-
    Revolutionary War Soldiers / Diane Smolinski.
        p. cm. -- (Americans at War: The Revolutionary War)
    Includes bibliographical references and index.
    ISBN 1-58810-276-9 (lib. bdg.)
    ISBN 978-1-58810-276-8 (HC)
    ISBN 1-58810-562-8 (pbk. bdg.)
    ISBN 978-1-58810-562-2 (PB)
    1. United States. Continental Army--History--
Juvenile literature. 2. United States. Continental
Army--Military life--Juvenile literature. 3. Soldiers--
United States--History--18th century--Juvenile literature.
4. Soldiers--United States--Social conditions--18th
century--Juvenile literature. 5. United States--History-
-Revolution, 1775-1783--Social aspects--Juvenile
literature. 6. United States--History--Revolution, 1775
-1783--American forces--Juvenile literature. [1. United
States. Continental Army. 2. United States--History--
Revolution, 1775-1783.] I. Title. II. Series: Smolinski,
Diane, 1950-   . Americans at war.
    Revolutionary War.
    E259.S66 2001
    973.3'4--dc21

                                    2001001620

Acknowledgments
The author and publishers are grateful to the
following for permission to reproduce copyright
material: p. 5, 7 top, 9, 11, 14 right, 16 bottom,
21, 22 The Granger Collection, New York; p.7
bottom, 8, 10, 12, 16 top, 18, 20, 23, 25, 26, 28
Peter Newark's Military Pictures; p. 13, 14, 24
Culver Pictures; p. 15 Bettmann/Corbis; p.17 Corbis;
p.19 top Courtesy, Illinois State Museum; p. 27, 29
North Wind Picture Archives.

Cover photograph © Peter Newark's Military Pictures

About the Author
Diane Smolinski is a teacher for the Seminole
County School District in Florida. She earned B.S.
of Education degrees from Duquesne University and
Slippery Rock University in Pennsylvania. For the past
fourteen years, Diane has taught the Revolutionary
War curriculum to fourth and fifth graders. Diane
has previously authored a series of Civil War books
for young readers. She lives with her husband, two
daughters, and their cat, Pepper.

Special thanks to Jim Fitch, a former Revolutionary
War reenactor, for the special interest he took in
sharing information.

About the Consultant
G.A. LoFaro is a lieutenant colonel in the U.S. Army
currently stationed at Fort McPherson, Georgia. After
graduating from West Point, he was commissioned in
the infantry. He has served in a variety of positions
in the 82nd Airborne Division, the Ranger Training
Brigade, and Second Infantry Division in Korea.
He has a Masters Degree in U.S. History from the
University of Michigan and is completing his Ph.D
in U.S. History at the State University of New York
at Stony Brook. He has also served six years on the
West Point faculty where he taught military history
to cadets.

Some words are shown in bold, **like this.**
You can find out what they mean by looking in the glossary.

Contents

Breaking Away from the British

When American colonists first started to talk about gaining independence from Great Britain, most did not want to break away from the rule of King George III. They had a trade agreement with Great Britain that was working well. The colonies sold raw materials to Great Britain, and Britain provided them with finished goods in return.

When Britain finished fighting the **French and Indian War** in 1763, the British government found itself in great debt. To raise money to pay this war debt, Britain passed tax laws in the colonies. These additional taxes upset many colonists. They did not want to have to give any more of their money to another country. A growing number of colonists were also thinking about governing themselves. In 1775, American and British government officials still had not reached an agreement about taxes or political rights. So, from 1775 to 1783, the British and colonial armies fought each other for control of the thirteen colonies.

The lives of the men who made laws in British Parliament were far removed from the lives of the colonists in North America. They could not understand why the colonists were so upset about being taxed by Great Britain.

Town Crier News

- In 1773, the Tea Act allowed a British company to sell tea in the colonies for a cheaper price than colonial merchants could. The colonial merchants were charged more taxes than the British companies, so they had to charge more for their product.

- In 1765, the Stamp Act required a tax to be paid when items such as documents, licenses, and newspapers were issued. The item was then stamped to show that the tax had been paid.

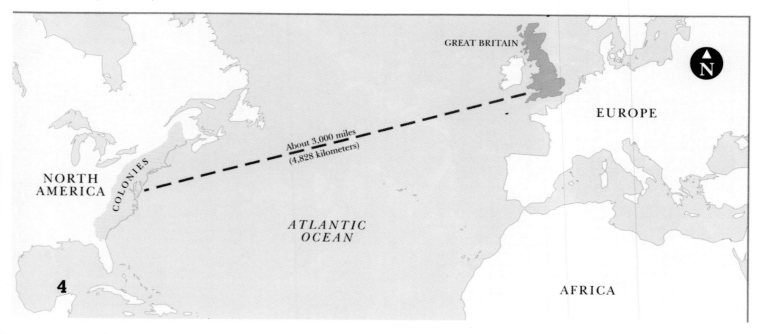

GREAT BRITAIN

N

EUROPE

NORTH AMERICA

COLONIES

About 3,000 miles (4,828 kilometers)

ATLANTIC OCEAN

AFRICA

The British Navy was important throughout the war because it transported troops and supplies and created blockades. The British Navy had approximately 30 warships and 400 transport ships.

The British Respond to Colonial Rebels

When the British government called for new taxes in the colonies, some citizens protested by not buying British products. In 1768, British troops traveled across the Atlantic Ocean to Boston, Massachusetts, to help stop these protests and to help Britain tighten its control over the government of Massachusetts. British Navy ships **blockaded** the seaport of Boston.

The British wanted to keep **Loyalists** in important political positions in the colonies to protect Britain's economic interests in North America. They did not want to settle these differences with fighting. However, in 1775, they found themselves going to war with the colonists to try to end these disagreements.

Town Crier News

On April 19, 1775, British troops and colonial **militiamen** exchanged musket fire in Lexington, Massachusetts. This was the start of the Revolutionary War.

Building Armies

At the beginning of the Revolutionary War, an army of British **regulars** fought against **militias,** made up of citizen soldiers, of the individual **colonies.** These colonial militiamen were no match for the disciplined, well-trained, and well-supplied British regular army.

The Continental Army

In June of 1775, the Continental Congress approved the formation of a national army. It was named the Continental Army. Congress called for the following:

> That six companies of expert rifflemen, be immediately raised in Pennsylvania, two in Maryland, and two in Virginia; that each company consist of a captain, three lieutenants, four serjeants, four corporals, a drummer or trumpeter, and sixty-eight privates.
> That each company, as soon as compleated, shall march and join the army near Boston, to be there employed as light infantry, under the command of the chief Officer in that army.

The Continental Army joined the militiamen to fight a growing regular British Army, foreign troops hired to fight for the British, and other forces loyal to Britain.

Continental Army troops wait in line for an inspection by General George Washington.

Town Crier News

- All physically fit men between the ages of 16 and 60 could serve in the state militias.

- Militiamen usually supplied their own equipment.

- In 1776, only 9,170 men had joined the Continental Army, even though Congress had authorized the army to have up to 20,372 men. This made the help of the state militias very important.

- On September 16, 1776, the Continental Congress authorized an Expanded Continental Army of 88 **battalions** to serve for the length of the war.

- Each of the thirteen colonies had to raise a specific number of battalions to contribute to this army.

- Massachusetts Bay Colony and Virginia had the highest **quotas.** They were to raise fifteen battalions each.

- Georgia and Delaware had the lowest quotas. Each only had to provide a single battalion.

Enlisting Continental Soldiers

In 1775, the Continental Congress established an **enlistment pledge** for the Continental soldier. It stated the following:

I _____ have, this day, voluntarily enlisted myself, as a soldier, in the American continental army, for one year, unless sooner discharged: And I do bind myself to conform, in all instances, to such rules and regulations, as are, or shall be, established for the government of the said Army.

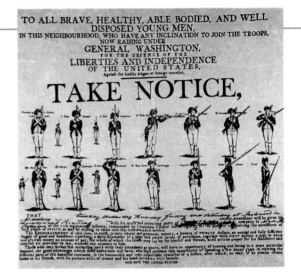

The Continental Army depended on volunteer soldiers. They used posters to try to attract new recruits.

The Continental Army had a hard time **recruiting** enough men. Congress set quotas for each state and could **draft** men if necessary. At first, soldiers enlisted for one year. After 1776, enlistments were for three years or until the war ended. When enlistment numbers were too low, states offered rewards of money and land to those who joined, but they still could not fill the quotas. Some states recruited slaves by promising them freedom from slavery in return for their service.

Gathering British Soldiers

The British already had an army and navy at the beginning of the
Revolutionary War. They needed to increase the size of their army because
they were also fighting and protecting territories in other parts of the world.
They decided to **recruit** men in England. There was much poverty in
England at this time, so men needing jobs were willing to join. They also
recruited **colonists** loyal to the British government, known as **Loyalists.**

Hessians

The British could not recruit enough soldiers in their own country and
in the colonies to protect all their territories scattered around the world.
Therefore, they arranged to hire troops from other countries, mainly from
the German state of Hesse Cassel. These men, called **Hessians,** were
experienced and disciplined soldiers.

Six German states sent nearly 30,000
soldiers to help the British fight the
Revolutionary War. The first of the
Hessian troops landed in New York
in August of 1776. They fought in all
parts of the colonies throughout the
war. At the end of the war, some of
these soldiers chose to stay in the
United States. Others went to live
in Canada or went back home.

*The British Army recruited Loyalist
volunteers in the North American
colonies by promising land in exchange
for their service.*

TEUCRO DUCE NIL DESPERANDOM.

First Battalion of PENNSYLVANIA LOYALISTS,
commanded by His Excellency Sir WILLIAM
HOWE, K B.

ALL INTREPID ABLE-BODIED

HEROES,

WHO are willing to serve His MAJESTY KING
GEORGE the Third, in Defence of their
Country, Laws and Constitution, against the arbitrary
Usurpations of a tyrannical Congress, have now not
only an Opportunity of manifesting their Spirit, by
assisting in reducing to Obedience their too-long de-
luded Countrymen, but also of acquiring the polite
Accomplishments of a Soldier, by serving only two
Years, or during the present Rebellion in America.
Such spirited Fellows, who are willing to engage,
will be rewarded at the End of the War, besides their
Laurels, with 50 Acres of Land, where every gallant
Hero may retire. . . . .
Each Volunteer will receive, as a Bounty, FIVE
DOLLARS, besides Arms, Cloathing and Accoutre-
ments, and every other Requisite proper to accommo-
date a Gentleman Soldier, by applying to Lieutenant
Colonel ALLEN, or at Captain KEARNY's Ren-
dezvous, at PATRICK TONRY's, three Doors above
Market-street, in Second-street.

Besides recruiting in the colonies, the British decided to increase the size of their army by hiring Hessians—soldiers from the German state of Hesse Cassel.

Town Crier News

- At the beginning of the Revolutionary War, there were about 8,000 British troops in North America.

- Due to its desperate need for more soldiers, the British Army offered some criminals the choice of joining the army instead of going to prison.

- Almost 17,000 men from the German state of Hesse Cassel came to the North American colonies to fight in the Revolutionary War for the British.

The Leaders

Congress **commissioned** the high-ranking officers of the Continental Army. Some came from state **militia** groups. Others were chosen because they held important political positions in their communities. Lower-ranking officers were selected by their states or **appointed** by the **commander in chief.** In 1775, the Continental Congress elected George Washington the first commander in chief of the Continental Army.

Leaders of the British Army

During the Revolutionary War, four men served as commander in chief of the British forces. British officers were also chosen in several ways. Some men from wealthy families paid to get positions as officers. They joined the military to gain power in the government and personal fame. Others who were not wealthy had to earn their positions based on their experience in the military.

General Horatio Gates was a Continental leader.   *Admiral Richard Earl helped lead the British.*

General George Washington (1732–1799)

George Washington served in the Virginia militia as early
as 1752. A few years later, he volunteered to help the British
defend land against the French. He took part in the first
engagement of the **French and Indian War** near the city of
Pittsburgh, Pennsylvania. In 1758, Washington resigned from
the military and went home to Virginia to manage his family's
tobacco plantation. The plantation was called Mount Vernon.

In 1774, Washington rejoined the Virginia militia to support the
revolutionaries against Great Britain. In June 1775, George Washington
was appointed general and commander in chief of the Continental Army.

*This 1772 oil painting shows George Washington as a colonel in the
Virginia militia.*

11

Town Crier News

- In 1776, the average private in the Continental Army received 6 2/3 Continental dollars per month. A colonel received $75 per month plus extra pay for food. Each soldier received an amount of supplies based on his rank.

- George Washington never accepted the $500 per month salary that Congress allowed him.

A Dedicated Military Leader

Throughout the Revolutionary War, George Washington encouraged his soldiers not to give up. He worked to train and organize his troops so they would be successful in battle. Washington tried to convince the political leaders to provide his soldiers with food, clothing, and enough pay to stay healthy so they would reenlist to continue fighting the war. When these basic needs were not met, it was very difficult for him to maintain a strong army.

George Washington takes command of the Continental Army in 1775.

Washington Time line

1750			1760
1752 Washington joins Virginia Militia	1753 Works for the British as a surveyor	1756 Becomes involved in the French and Indian War	

George Washington says goodbye to the officers of the Continental Army.

The End of a Military Career

Once the war ended, Washington gave a farewell speech to the Continental Army on November 2, 1783. In this speech, he stated the following:

> To the various branches of the Army the General takes this last and solemn opportunity ... to bid a final adieu to the Armies he has so long had the honor to Command ... the Commander in Chief is about to retire from Service.

On December 23, 1783, George Washington officially resigned his **commission** as **commander in chief** and returned home to Virginia.

Looking Ahead

General Washington realized the importance of a ready military force, even during peacetime. He encouraged leaders to build up a **regular** army, a **militia,** multiple **arsenals,** and military academies. Eventually, many of his ideas became realities. Today, the United States is known for the strength of its Armed Forces.

Town Crier News

- Today, the U.S. has a regular standing force of military personnel in the Army, Navy, Air Force, and Marines. The Coast Guard becomes part of the Navy during wartime.

- Arsenals were established, which today are training sites for the military.

- Military academies were eventually established at West Point, New York, for the Army; Annapolis, Maryland, for the Navy and the Marine Corp; Colorado Springs, Colorado, for the Air Force; and in New London, Connecticut, for the Coast Guard.

1770		1780
1774 Rejoins the Virginia State Militia	**1775 Commissioned as commander in chief of the Continental Army**	**1783 Resigns his commission and returns home to Virginia**

Friedrich von Steuben

(1730–1794)

On February 23, 1778, a German soldier named Friedrich Wilhelm von Steuben came from Europe to help General Washington train Continental troops at Valley Forge, Pennsylvania. Von Steuben had served in the German Army under Frederick the Great. He immediately recognized that the Continental troops needed discipline and training to fight effectively against the British Army.

Town Crier News

- Von Steuben offered to serve without pay.

- He was **appointed** Inspector General in charge of training the Continental Army.

- He spoke little English, yet he was able to train the English-speaking troops.

Von Steuben taught groups of men to march, take care of their weapons, and use a **bayonet.** These men then taught others. Von Steuben wrote a manual of arms, or a training book of directions, so everyone would learn to do things the same way. After several months of training with von Steuben, the Continental soldiers were more confident and better prepared to face the British Army.

Von Steuben's manual of arms was used in the United States Army until the War of 1812.

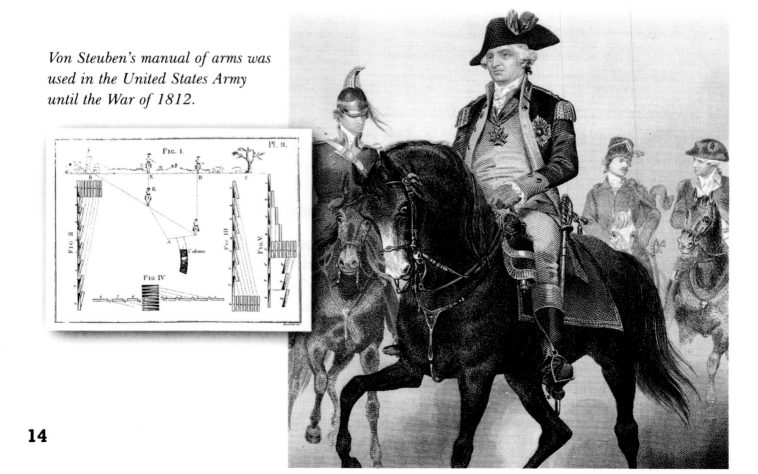

Commanders in Chief of the British Army

Four important British generals brought leadership and experience to the battlefields during the Revolutionary War. Their names were Thomas Gage, Sir William Howe, Sir Henry Clinton, and Sir Guy Carleton.

General Thomas Gage

Thomas Gage was born and educated in England. He was a professional soldier in the British Army. Gage served in the **French and Indian War,** which was fought from 1754 to 1763, and then he became the first **commander in chief** of the British forces in the **colonies.** Gage returned to England for a short time before the Revolutionary War began. He came back to the colonies in 1774 and was reappointed commander in chief of the British forces. Despite his victory at the Battle of Bunker Hill in 1775, he was ordered to return to England. British government officials were unhappy with him for not putting an end to the protests in the colonies.

Town Crier News

• Thomas Gage served as governor of Montreal, Canada, in 1760.

• He was governor of the colony of Massachusetts in 1774.

General Gage is shown here in a regional British military uniform. This uniform identified him as the commander of a particular unit.

General Sir William Howe

When General Gage was ordered to return to England, Sir William Howe became the **commander in chief** of the British forces. Howe won several battles and took over Philadelphia, but British officials were upset that he failed to win the war quickly. After three years, General Sir Henry Clinton replaced Howe.

General Sir Henry Clinton

Sir Henry Clinton was born into a wealthy British family. In 1775, he received orders to come to North America to help stop the **rebellion.** That same year, he became second in command of the British forces under General Howe. In 1778, General Clinton replaced Howe as commander in chief of the British forces in the American **colonies.** After four years of fighting, Clinton was unable to completely defeat the colonists. He turned his command over to General Sir Guy Carleton and returned to England.

General Sir Henry Clinton captured New York and Rhode Island for the British in 1778.

General Sir William Howe directs the departure of British troops from the city of Boston in 1776.

Commanders Time line

1740	1750	1760	1770
1740 Gage joins the British Army.	**1755** Gage comes to North America to serve in the French and Indian War.	**1763** Gage becomes commander in chief of British forces in the colonies.	**1774** Gage returns to North America from England and again becomes commander in chief of British forces in the colonies.

General Sir Guy Carleton

Sir Guy Carleton first served in the British Army in North America during the **French and Indian War.** When Thomas Gage resigned, Carleton commanded the British forces in Canada. In 1782, after the British surrendered, Carleton was **appointed** the commander in chief of British forces in the colonies. He was in charge of stopping the fighting and removing the British forces from the colonies. He was also to help the **Loyalists** either leave or resettle in their old homes, depending on what each person chose to do.

British **Parliament** was under pressure to end the war quickly and begin trading with the colonies again. Gage, Howe, Clinton, and Carleton were all good leaders, but none of them was able to end the war as quickly as Parliament expected. Therefore, their commands were shortened by Parliament.

*When fighting broke out in Massachusetts, General Sir Guy Carleton sent his Canadian **regulars** to Boston to help the British.*

Town Crier News

- Sir William Howe was a member of the British Parliament from 1758 to 1780.

- Sir Henry Clinton started his military career as a soldier in the New York State **Militia.** His father, Admiral George Clinton, was the governor of New York in 1741.

- Sir Guy Carleton was the governor of Quebec, Canada, before and after the Revolutionary War.

1770			1780
1775 Howe becomes commander in chief of British forces in the colonies.	**1775** Clinton comes to the colonies from England to help stop the rebellion. He becomes second in command to Howe.	**1778** Clinton becomes commander in chief of British forces in the colonies.	**1782** Carleton becomes commander in chief of British forces in the colonies.

Infantry

Most soldiers in the British and Continental Armies served in the infantry. These foot soldiers marched in columns to the sound of drums and fifes and fought shoulder to shoulder in a battle line. Infantrymen generally marched from battle to battle. If they needed to travel long distances, they used boats.

British infantrymen had better equipment to use in hand-to-hand combat and had more training than Continental soldiers. The maximum number of men allowed in an infantry **regiment** in the Continental Army was set at 608. The maximum number of men in a British infantry regiment was 477.

Equipment

Equipment was essential for the infantrymen to survive. Soldiers needed uniforms, weapons, boots, blankets, tents, eating utensils, **canteens, cartridge** boxes, and **haversacks.** Since the Continental Army was put together quickly, the government did not have the time or money to supply an entire army of soldiers with proper equipment. Soldiers often wore their own clothing and brought their own weapons. The wealthier British government was better able to equip its soldiers.

Town Crier News

- Canteens were made of wood and tin.

- Soldiers had to stand up to load their large muskets.

- A British flintlock musket weighed 4 pounds (6 kilograms) and was 42 inches (1 meter) long.

Weapons

The **flintlock musket** was the weapon used by both armies at the beginning of the war. It shot musket balls. A **bayonet** was attached to the end of the barrel. Since the musket was inaccurate at a range of more than 50 yards (46 meters), the bayonet was actually the most effective weapon of the infantryman.

A well-trained soldier could load and shoot three times, or rounds, in one minute.

Feeding the Soldiers

The armies often did not have money to purchase food for the soldiers. **Inflation** made food very expensive. Farmers and merchants did not always accept **colonial** paper money, and wagons often were not available to transport supplies or could not catch up with troops on the move. Hungry soldiers were forced to search for food in the surrounding fields and forests.

Patriot troops at the Battle of Guilford Court House fire muskets and charge with bayonets.

Artillery

Men in both armies were trained to fire and maintain cannons called artillery. The men, cannons, equipment, and horses together were called a battery.

Field Artillery

Field cannons moved with the infantry as the foot soldiers attacked an enemy position. A cannon could be attached to a two-wheeled wooden frame for horses or oxen to pull to the battlefield. Horse-drawn wagons carried the ammunition. A crew of soldiers firing a cannon had to find the target, estimate, or guess, the distance the cannonball needed to travel, and select the proper ammunition. Artillery fire could destroy attacking troops moving across open ground or protect troops defending a fixed position.

Continental Army artillerymen managed the field artillery cannons.

Town Crier News

- Revolutionary War cannons were made of cast iron or brass.

- The Continental Army did not have its own cannons at the beginning of the war. It used British cannons left over from the **French and Indian War.**

- Artillery was sized by the weight of the shells. Shells could weigh 3, 6, 9, 12, or 24 pounds (1, 3, 4, 5, or 11 kilograms).

- Soldiers who manned the cannons were called gunners and bombardiers.

Henry Knox was selected as the Chief of Artillery of the Continental Army. He learned about artillery from reading British books on this subject.

Garrison and Siege Artillery

Garrison and siege artillery were larger types of cannons. Garrison, or fortress, cannons were positioned at a fort to protect the fort from an attacking army or to control important river positions.

Siege cannons were used against an enemy that was trapped or surrounded. They were big and heavy and could not be moved easily. Siege cannons fired larger-sized cannonballs that traveled longer distances than field artillery. These cannons were used to attack fortifications and buildings.

Cavalry

Cavalry soldiers rode horses. Cavalry units were small compared to the number of foot soldiers in an infantry unit. They rode ahead of the infantry to gather information about the opposing army. They also patrolled the outside edges of the army.

Riding horses, cavalry soldiers could travel long distances quickly and attack without warning. The **saber** was the most effective weapon of the cavalry rider, but soldiers also carried pistols and **carbines.**

On January 17, 1781, at the Battle of Cowpens, 80 Continental cavalry soldiers led by George Washington's cousin William helped defeat the British force.

The Continental Cavalry

The Continental dragoons were cavalry units of the Continental Army. Throughout the war, Congress asked for several cavalry **regiments** to be formed. No cavalry regiment had more than 30 men. Units often did not have enough horses for everyone because they were expensive and hard to find. Cavalry units called legions had some mounted troops and some troops on foot. Lee's Legion, commanded by Colonel Henry "Light Horse Harry" Lee, was one of the most famous of these units.

The British Cavalry

The British cavalry troops, also called dragoons, were well-disciplined, trained soldiers who protected the British columns when they were marching from place to place. Lieutenant Colonel Banastre Tarleton was a famous British cavalry leader. He became known for his brutal treatment of his enemies.

The Fourteenth Light Dragoon was just one of the British cavalry units serving in the Revolutionary War. A member of that unit is pictured here.

Uniforms

Uniforms of the Continental Army

The North American **colonies** did not have many factories that made clothing. The British Navy was blocking port cities, so getting uniforms from Europe was nearly impossible. At the beginning of the war, Continental soldiers wore many different designs of uniforms. Cavalry troops had uniforms. They often wore fringed hunting shirts and leggings. They may have worn helmets for protection.

The first official uniform color was brown, but different **regiments** wore different colors. In 1779, the army chose a single official color. Infantry coats were blue and trimmed with different colors to identify a particular state or region. Officers wore colored **sashes,** ribbons, and **rosettes** over their clothing.

Continental troops had a wide variety of uniforms during the Revolutionary War.

Town Crier News

- Infantry regiments in New England wore blue coats with white trim. Soldiers in New York and New Jersey wore blue coats with a yellowish brown trim. Soldiers in Pennsylvania, Delaware, Maryland, and Virginia wore blue coats with red trim. Regiments in North Carolina, South Carolina, and Georgia wore blue coats with a blue trim edged in white.

- In 1778, the French sent some blue and brown coats with red trim to the colonial troops. That was the largest group of uniforms of the same design used by the Continental Army up to that point in the war.

Cavalry troops wore the reverse colors of those worn by the infantry so they could be spotted easily when they were needed. Artillery uniforms were blue coats with scarlet, or bright red, trim.

Uniforms of the British Army

The British Army had very formal uniforms. The uniforms were designed to allow soldiers to march, shoot, and charge in large, open spaces. However, they often seemed too heavy and bulky for the British troops to chase Continental troops over mountains or through thick forests.

A private in the British Army wore a red topcoat with a red or white **waistcoat** underneath. White trousers, or pants, were fastened near the top of the calf. A **cartridge** belt was worn over the left shoulder. A **bayonet** was attached to a thin belt around the waist. A knapsack, **haversack,** blanket, tent equipment, and a musket completed the uniform.

Taking care of their uniforms and equipment was a never-ending chore for the British soldiers. Brass buttons, buckles, and shoes had to be shined, belts needed to be kept white, and guns had to be kept clean.

Town Crier News

- British infantrymen wore red waistcoats, but all other troops wore white waistcoats.

- The British soldiers were nicknamed "redcoats" because of the red color of the coats of their infantry uniforms.

This is a typical uniform of a British "redcoat" during the war.

Comparing Forces

Similarities

The newly formed Continental Army was similar to the British Army in several ways. Most of the soldiers in both armies were infantrymen. Light artillery units followed and supported these foot soldiers wherever they marched. Both armies used mainly muskets, **bayonets,** and light field guns for weapons.

Some Continental soldiers fought with the British in the **French and Indian War,** so they had learned to drill and fight as the British soldiers did. They learned to march from place to place in columns and to line up shoulder to shoulder in rows to fire muskets and attack with bayonets. But despite similarities between the two armies, it took years of training before the Continental soldier had the skills to match the British soldier.

Differences

Even though the Continental Army was modeled after the British Army, the two were very different when the Revolutionary War started. The British were much better prepared to fight a war. The British Army was made up of full-time soldiers. They trained daily with the same group of men

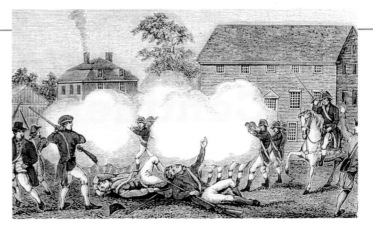

Massachusetts militiamen defended the town of Lexington against British regular troops.

and were very disciplined. Many British soldiers and officers had years of military service and experience before the Revolutionary War began.

The Continental Army was formed mainly from part-time volunteers in state **militia** groups. **Colonial** men were often more concerned with their farms and businesses than with being soldiers. They had to learn to work together and make the army their full-time job. Some Continental officers had served with the British in the French and Indian War, but most colonial soldiers had served less than one year in a state militia unit and did not have any war experience.

Infantrymen at the Battle of Bunker Hill marched in rows, or ranks, two or three deep. Officers marched behind the ranks and gave commands.

Tough Times for the Continental Soldier

"These are the times that try men's souls."
—**Thomas Paine in *The American Crisis*, a series of essays about his experiences in the Continental Army**

The conditions at Valley Forge, Pennsylvania, during the winter of 1777–1778 proved how hard life could be for the Continental soldier. The troops arrived without shoes, warm clothing, or blankets, and the weather turned cold, windy, and snowy. Supplies of food and clothing did not come as needed. Nearly 900 log huts had to be built for the soldiers. Hundreds of soldiers became ill from typhus, smallpox, pneumonia, and malnutrition. Many died. The men who survived began to train under General Friedrich von Steuben, the German soldier appointed by General Washington to teach the troops. The **colonists** had a lot of work to do if they hoped to win this war.

At first, colonial soldiers often did not fight in the traditional battle lines, but stayed hidden behind trees, fences, and buildings. This type of fighting helped the smaller colonial forces compete with the larger British forces.

Town Crier News

- George Washington lived in a tent like the other soldiers until log huts were being built for his men. He then moved into a stone house on the property.

- Martha Washington, George's wife, came to Valley Forge in February 1778. She helped organize some entertainment for the troops.

- More than 1,500 **engagements** were fought during the Revolutionary War.

After suffering defeats at the Battles of Brandywine and Germantown, the Continental Army marched to Valley Forge for the winter to rest and train. The harsh winter brought down the numbers of the army even more.

Winning the War

From the first battle at Lexington, Massachusetts, in 1775, to the final surrender at Yorktown, Virginia, in 1783, soldiers bravely fought many difficult battles in the Revolutionary War. Common citizens, professional soldiers, Native Americans, and foreign troops battled on land, rivers, lakes, the Atlantic Ocean, and on the frontier.

The soldiers often faced cold weather, hunger, and exhaustion. They did not have medicine, proper clothing, and shelter. These difficult conditions caused more soldiers to die from disease and illness than from battle wounds. But it was through the courage of these soldiers that a government free from British control was born.

Glossary

appoint   to elect to an office or position of authority

arsenal   collection of weapons and other military equipment

battalion   large military unit of two or more batteries acting together

battery   artillery unit of men, cannons, equipment, and horses

bayonet   long, pointed knife that attached to the end of a musket or rifle

blockade   troops or warships that block enemy troops or supplies from entering or leaving an area

canteen   container that a soldier used for carrying drinking water

carbine   rifle with a short barrel

cartridge   small container that held gunpowder and bullets

colony   territory settled by people from other countries who still had loyalty to those other countries. The word *colonist* is used to describe a person who lives in a colony. The word *colonial* is used to describe things related to a colony.

commander in chief   highest ranking official in charge of all the military forces

commission   to officially give a rank in the military

draft   to require men to join the military

engagement   any fighting occurring during a war

enlistment pledge   official promise made when signing up for the military

fife   small flute

flintlock musket   type of gun with a long barrel where a hard stone called flint would strike against a piece of steel on the gun. This produced a spark that made the gunpowder explode.

French and Indian War   called the Seven Years' War in Europe. From 1754 to 1763, Britain fought against France in the North American colonies. Some Native Americans—called Indians at the time—helped the French.

haversack   linen bag usually worn over the shoulder that held a soldier's food rations

Hessian   soldier from the German state of Hesse Cassel

inflation   increase in the usual price of goods

Loyalist   colonist who supported the British government during the American Revolution

militia   group of ordinary men who fought to protect the colonies before the Revolutionary War and then fought alongside the Continental Army during the war

Parliament   lawmakers of the British government

quota   set number of soldiers a state was supposed to enlist

rebellion   act of trying to take over a legal government

recruit   to persuade people to sign up for something, usually military service

regiment   group of soldiers

regular   full-time soldier

rosette   ribbon decoration shaped like a rose worn on an officer's uniform

saber   sword used by the cavalry

sash   wide piece of material worn around the waist

waistcoat   soldier's vest

Historical Fiction to Read

Gregory, Kristiana. *The Winter of Red Snow: The Revolutionary War Diary of Abigail Jane Stewart.* New York: Scholastic, 1998.
Eleven-year-old Abigail presents a diary account of life in Valley Forge from December 1777 to July 1778 as General Washington prepares his troops to fight the British.

Osborne, Mary Pope. *Revolutionary War on Wednesday.* New York: Random House, 2000.
Kids travel back in time to the Revolutionary War to help General Washington during the Delaware River Crossing.

Historical Places to Visit

Boston National Historical Park
Charlestown Navy Yard
Boston, Massachusetts 02129-4543
Visitor Information: (617) 242-5642
Take the Freedom Trail walking tour of the park to see sixteen Revolutionary War sites and structures. Visit downtown Boston to see the Old State House and the Paul Revere House. Visit Charlestown to see the Bunker Hill Monument.

Colonial National Historical Park
P.O. Box 210
Yorktown, Virginia 23690
Visitor Information: (757) 898-2410
Visit Yorktown, the site of the last major battle of the Revolutionary War in 1781.

Minute Man National Historical Park
174 Liberty Street
Concord, Massachusetts 01742
Visitor Information: (978) 369-6993
This park stretches across the historic sites of some of the opening battles of the Revolutionary War. Visit the sites of the battles at Concord, Lincoln, and Lexington.

Valley Forge National Historical Park
P.O. Box 953
Valley Forge, Pennsylvania 9482-0953
Visitor Information: (610) 783-1077
Visit the place where Friedrich von Steuben trained George Washington's Continental Army during the winter of 1777 to 1778.

Index